Shared Sightings

Shared Sightings

An Anthology of Bird Poems

edited by
Sheila Golburgh Johnson

drawings by Katy Peake

John Daniel & Company, Santa Barbara, 1995

Printed in the United States of America

Published by John Daniel and Company
A division of Daniel and Daniel, Publishers, Inc.
Post Office Box 21922
Santa Barbara, CA 93121

Cover art by Katy Peake
Cover design by Kath Christensen

LIBRARY OF CONGRESS CATALOGING-IN-PUBLICATION DATA
Shared sightings : an anthology of bird poems / edited by Sheila Golburgh Johnson
p. cm.
ISBN 1-880284-12-X
1. Birds—poetry. 2. American poetry—20th century. I. Johnson, Sheila Golburgh.
PS595.B5S53 1995
811'.5408036—dc20
94-39717
CIP

To my father
with love

Contents

All Morning

Random Sightings

Nightwatch

Preface

A female cardinal lit on a privet hedge as I passed and cocked her head at me while I stared. "What now?" she seemed to ask. It was the day after my mother died, when I had walked endless miles through the leafy suburbs of my hometown, hoping for the oblivion of exhaustion. At the time the bird seemed to be a messenger from my mother, and the image remains in my memory as the only sweet note I heard in those sad days.

Who can imagine a world without birds? One poet included here did imagine it in "What if?", but having imagined it, could not leave the world so empty. By the end of the poem, the "first bird of the universe…" makes an appearance. Birds have been part of our collective consciousness since our time on earth began. Language itself, the gift that makes us most human, is mythically connected to birds as Vladimir Nabokov mentions in his poem, "An Evening of Russian Poetry":

> *On mellow hills the Greek, as you remember,*
> *fashioned his alphabet from cranes in flight….*

A different vision of this bird's gift informs "A Quest for Cranes," one of the poems collected here.

This anthology gathers the work of thirty-five poets who gaze at the spiritual horizon between humans and the rest of nature, and find a reflection of their deepest concerns; who understand that animal life may not always be measured by human standards. In a world much older than the one we know the birds fly complete with senses we have lost, living by voices we hear only in brief melody. They are neither a lower order of life nor are they our equals; they are another nation caught in the inevitable thrust of geologic time and bound, as we are, to earth's bounty and splendor.

Some birds, such as hawks, owls, and crows, appear in many of the poems, but the responses to these birds are as different as the light lining each poet's inner eye. Some birds appear only once, having caught a poet's fancy with a glimpse into the secret heart of nature. Why a poet chooses one bird or another for a poem is as mysterious as why people fall in love.

I wish to thank the poets, without whom this anthology would not be; Katy Peake, the artist who gave generously of her talent; the publishers, John and Susan Daniel, who believed in the book; and D. Barton Johnson, who knows birds.

—SHEILA GOLBURGH JOHNSON

All Morning

All Morning

Here in our aging district the wood pigeon lives with us,
His deep-throated cooing part of the early morning,
Far away, close-at-hand, his call floating over the on-coming traffic,
The lugubriously beautiful plaint uttered at regular intervals,
A protest from the past, a reminder.

They sit, three or four, high in the fir-trees back of the house,
Flapping away heavily when a car blasts too close,
And one drops down to the garden, the high rhododendron,
Only to fly over to his favorite perch, the cross-bar of a telephone
pole;
Grave, hieratic, a piece of Assyrian sculpture,
A thing carved of stone or wood, with the dull iridescence of long-
polished wood,
Looking at you without turning his small head,
With a round vireo's eye, quiet and contained,
Part of the landscape.

And the Stellar jay, raucous, sooty headed, lives with us,
Conducting his long wars with the neighborhood cats,
All during mating season,
Making a racket to wake the dead,
To distract attention from the short-tailed ridiculous young ones
Hiding deep in the blackberry bushes—
What a scuttling and rapping along the drainpipes,
A fury of jays, diving and squawking,
When our spayed female cat yawns and stretches out in the
sunshine—
And the wrens scold, and the chickadees frisk and frolic,
Pitching lightly over the high hedgerows, dee-deeing,

And the ducks near Lake Washington waddle down the highway
after a rain,
Stopping traffic, indignant as addled old ladies,
Pecking at crusts and peanuts, their green necks glittering;
And the hummingbird dips in and around the quince tree,
Veering close to my head,
Then whirring off sideways to the top of the hawthorn,
Its almost-invisible wings, buzzing, hitting the loose leaves
intermittently—

A delirium of birds!
Peripheral dippers come to rest on the short grass,
Their heads jod-jodding like pigeons;
The gulls, the gulls far from their waves
Rising, wheeling away with harsh cries,
Coming down on a patch of lawn:

It is neither spring nor summer: it is Always,
With towhees, finches, chickadees, California quail, wood doves,
With wrens, sparrows, juncos, cedar waxwings, flickers,
With Baltimore orioles, Michigan bobolinks,
And those birds forever dead,
The passenger pigeon, the great auk, the Carolina paraquet,
All birds remembered, O never forgotten!
All in my yard, of a perpetual Sunday,
All morning! All morning!

Of Wings

Angels have eagles' wings
Renaissance paintings
conferred on them
or is it eagles angels?
Each makes a big tempting
target but an angel
the instant it is felled
resurrects whereas an eagle
once shot soon grows cold.

Angels subsist on ambrosia.
Eagles mainly on fish.
It is rumored that an eagle
will uplift a newborn lamb
but six lbs. is as much as
it can fly with whereas angels
as stolid as ants or oxen
can team up to displace
many times their body mass.

While Rilke's radiant vision
in every elegy sustained
him, what Benjamin Franklin
thought of angels is not known
but he declared the eagle
a bird of bad moral
character and proposed
the wild turkey instead
for our national symbol.

Wild is not the same as free.
The turkey's inability
to soar puts it upon
the ceremonial table
every Thanksgiving
thereby sparing eagles
or angels, both of whom
on attaining great heights
endure intense cold. Eagles

scarce elsewhere although
common as seagulls
above the dump at Juneau
when basking on air
between voracious forays
as graceful as angels
are objects to admire
nevertheless and will be
as long as we let them fly

while glorious angels
draped in genderless glitter
unseen as the souls
they purport to carry
excite us to be better
than we are before
they take us wingless and unsure
far beyond eagles
to the lockup in the sky.

Hosanna

We looked up at the passing of wings
and neither could name them.
Although you tried to key them
from your book of birds,
I knew you wouldn't find them there.
Suddenly their shapes
seemed to fill with light
and when I cried out,
for an instant illumined as they,
you said it was merely a shaft of sun
in my eyes. But I knew
as surely as the morning remembrance
of a dream what I had seen,
and in that glimpse of glory
I thrust you away with my silence
and listened to my heart
singing their hymn.

This Sparrow's Story

There it was, printed large as a mouse turd
in the newspaper the man dropped
right in front of my left eye:
Sparrows are trash birds
and me a sparrow.

How do you suppose I felt
being publicly classed with the world's garbage?
I'm as proud as the next bird, even counting
those conceited divas, the nightingales,
who sing for hire when commanded
by the Royals. I mean I care
that I am as winged as any
and fly on the same winds,
nourish my dear little self on the same seeds,
skimming the tops of wheat with artistry and élan,
dip-diving with ultimate grace.
But I am not here to convince, just to tell.

Don't imagine I didn't notate the name
of that basher, and elected a cockroach
to case the news office for his address
which he did with alacrity,
admiring my style and status.
The summons went out the next morning
to the multitudes of my look-alikes;
sparrows all, and we gathered
on this personality's roof
and orchestrated ourselves
into a cacophony that drowned out
all possibility of human conversation,

thought, or inner serenity.
In teams as disciplined as regiments
we chattered and cheeped and crazed him,
until on the third day
he caved in and fled the town forever.
Thus I erased the epithet
to my extreme satisfaction
and that of my fellow flyers
and, knowing our power,
we now are the ones who book
the nightingales into the Royals' gardens
to sweeten their summer evenings
and our own treasury with profitable contentment.

Moral: Offend a sparrow at your own risk.

So Many Sparrows

So many sparrows teaching
this morning to fly
with wing and diversion,
keeping me safe, in their scatter,
from reforming the night birds
of darkness I breathed through just barely
before the sun opened my eyes.
So many voices lodged in their throats;
schoolyard and meadow
welcome and anger
words round those tables
where never much pleasure
provided a balance.
Sing onward, brief birds,
I'll not score your notes
that flitter the air
but I listen to each
all together as one,
and seize my salvation
as your presence surrounds
the confines of now
this hour of morning
chance prelude to change.

Fishing the Sky

Once the heron sets
sail its shadow
harrows the tide-
pools, the shallows.
Soapy foam fills
each seep it waded.
Risen, the bird
outreaches the broken
beach (ripe bushes
no bill probes
for berries).
                    Snaps
shellfish aloft…
Lets them plummet,
splatter the rocks.

Diving, devours them.

Windward it wanders—
The sun a net
to drag below
its gaze.   (Trolling,
it awaits the least
flash,
        flicker
of scale or fin
in a trough.)
                    Slowly
rows its wings,
fishing the sky
over the shadow-
crossed shore,
the glimmering sea.

The Strolling Crow

for Bob Brill

I

Clumping along down the college path
like a proper man on a morning stroll
comes a cocky crow, as wide a crow
and tall and sleek and true a crow
as you'd ever see.

As nice a crow as I'll ever be.

I didn't expect to meet a crow
in just that way.
Pompous crow: pushy crow:
sharp and fat as a muscle-flex.
Left-step out, peck-glance, step right:
humorous crow: neighborly crow:
focus of light. Disinterested light.

But goodness knows, the cause of the crow's
strange strolling here
is clear as clear:

A crow can't hover
in the empty air
forever.

2

Crows on the highway, nailing down
a sometimes rabbit.
Crows on the housetops. Crows on the lawn.
Beaks rivet.
Kin to vulture, raven, kite.
But crows are gayer.
This strolling crow, he passes like
an overseer.

Who'd expect a crow so wise
he'd nod? Implausible.
Come strolling crow, crow civilized,
anything's possible!

3

I'll take a crow for my emblem beast
in the game we play, "Reveal Your Soul,"
at faculty parties. Even though
the Grand Massif, moustached and piped,
who teaches history—man you'd think
would act the lion—speaks
Gazelle,
few'd choose a crow. Not even though
our loveliest lady's known to pick
pike in the lake, and once a snake
—she was tired that night, she was feeling like a saint;
she was dreaming of the sun on her saurian back—

but a *crow*?

4

That's me, that's me, purebred crow,
black as a splinter of anthracite coal,
bumpy old umbrella in a fumbly wind,
hard without if soft within,
sure and clean as a painted skull
and shiny as a pocket comb:
bothered by a stuffed shirt:
awkward as a torn sheet
flopping on the laundry line—
rinsowhite turned insideout—an

honest creature:
rapacious in my nature:
formal dress: an agile eye:
clumping down the college path,
glancing right, glancing left:

what bird he'd be may mean the life
or the death of a man. Old crow,
pass on!

Crow babies

The crows are scolding the hunters.
The crows are calling me out
under the oaks to attend to them.
They like me, I am useful,
they flap near my shoulders and feet
large as dogs with wings.
They are always on patrol.

They bless me.
They let me hear them sing
an opera in the pitch pines.
They have many cries
and their eyes are jackknives
and their feathers carved
of obsidian and rainbows.

They raise their children
on my land, another blessing.
This year I watched them teaching
flight, big awkward children
like overgrown corner boys
cursing at top decibel,
tumbling, ruffled, pissed.

Why do we have to learn this,
they keep complaining, why
can't you go on feeding us?
Do you want to crawl like her,
the parents, the aunts,
the grandmothers mocked them,
when men chase you, you'll fly.

I scatter corn in the winter.
They squat on my compost pile
steaming into the snow and jeer
at lesser birds and tell ribald
jokes and laugh. They ignore
my cats who ignore them.
Now the year's offspring

are furled into huge black
umbrellas, bumbershoots, dressed
the same as their parents
like Hasidics. They share food,
they post guards, they fight
owls together: a better society
in the interstices of ours.

We speak of seeing the heron, as if there were only one

it by an incoming front,
gg, half rumpled frost clouds,
ooth, grooved only with the wakes
ped out onto the dike marching
grees, clear and still,
brandy igniting the brain.

down on the roadway,
eron, lord of the marsh,
ncer, the totem of this place
s bright light blood.
e bank but he was frozen
think at sunset.

I was stropped with rage against the fool
who answered strange beauty by killing it.
I see herons in afternoon pumpkin light
flapping up the Herring River, by the Inn
at Duck Creek, I see them at sunset landing
with a little stiff drop on their marshy isle.

But dawn is when they stand as omens to me,
the biggest near to the dike, guarding the flock
that feeds in stippled shallows the tide has bared.
Any day I see you begins blessed, for I pray
by walking, making my nishmat*, and your wide
wings promise me something holy survives.

**morning prayer in Judaism*

The West Main Book Store chickens

Always a shock:
like biting into a waxy golden
apple that shines like the harvest moon
and finding it mush.
In diners, in restaurants squatting at the end of motels
breathing liquory air, I order eggs.
The first bite lies on my tongue
rubbery as a bathing cap.

O eggs of Joanna's chickens,
your yolks are yellow as April sunshine.
Yellow as daffodil trumpets.
Sweet as sweet butter.
Your whites are clear and fragrant,
bowls of shad blossoms.

Joanna's chickens all have names.
They can fly. You look at them
and they cock their heads and look back.
Their manure feeds my cucumbers.
Gemma picks them up to talk to, hen
tucked under her arm like a fat puppy.
One bronze rooster gleams.
Quiches tender as rose petals,
mayonnaise you could grow fat admiring:
real chickens lay real eggs.

Art for art's sake

My walk on the tracks I measure in mockingbird
territories, passing through each virtuoso's
recital, like going down a conservatory hall

past practice rooms. I want to know what
evolutionary advance or sexual selection
has led to this oral patchwork of mimicry.

I can accept the imitation of seaside
sparrow, jay, gull, goldfinch, thrush;
but a green frog sitting at the top of a rum

cherry tree? Is it to thrill his mate
I have heard him give a creditable try
at a rototiller turning over a garden?

City Sounds

Between bulldozers
and powersaws
competing
with motorbikes and jets
almost outshouted
by sirens and train whistles
a mockingbird
perches
on the tip of a peach tree
and preaches
music

How Could I Have Forgotten

How could I have forgotten
that my roots entwine
with those of the tall Eucalyptus
where the raw calling
of a hawk for its mate
echoes wild eons
in my memory?

Why did I not know
when wind blew
scents of summer fields
into my face
that I could soar with it
to those sweet poppies
weaving like crimson butterflies
among the ripening wheat?

Why did the taste of water
cold on my tongue
not flood me with waves
buoyant as the ones
that floated me into being?

Why did I let escape
that silver balloon
the link between me
and the clouds
and when did I first pretend
I can not fly?

Night Herons

Night herons nest in the cypress
by the San Francisco
stationary boilers
with the high smoke stack
at the edge of the waters:
a steam turbine pump
to drive salt water
into the city's veins
mains
if the earth ever
quakes. and the power fails.
and water
to fight fire, runs
loose on the streets
with no pressure.

At the wire gate tilted slightly out
the part-wolf dog
would go in, to follow
if his human buddy lay on his side
and squirmed up first.

An abandoned, decaying, army.
a rotten rusty island prison
surrounded by lights of whirling
fluttering god-like birds
who truth
has never forgot.

I walk with my wife's sister
past the frozen bait;
with a long-bearded architect,
my dear brother,
and silent friend, whose
moustache curves wetly into his mouth
and he sometimes bites it.

the dog knows no laws and is strictly,
illegal. His neck arches and ears prick out
to catch mice in the tundra.
a black high school boy
drinking coffee at a fake green stand
tries to be friendly with the dog,
and it works.

How could the
night herons ever come back?
to this noisy place on the bay.
like me.
the joy of all the beings
is in being
older and tougher and eaten
up.
in the tubes and lanes of things
in the sewers of bliss and judgment,
in the glorious cleansing
treatment
plants.

We pick our way
through the edge of the city
early
subtly spreading changing sky;

ever-fresh and lovely dawn.

Magpie's Song

Six A.M.,
Sat down on excavation gravel
by juniper and desert S.P. tracks
interstate 80 not far off
        between trucks
Coyotes—maybe three
            howling and yapping from a rise.

Magpie on a bough
Tipped his head and said,

"Here in the mind, brother
Turquoise blue.
I wouldn't fool you.
Smell the breeze
It came through all the trees
No need to fear
What's ahead
Snow up on the hills west
Will be there every year
be at rest.
A feather on the ground—
The wind sound—

Here in the Mind, Brother,
Turquoise Blue"

Buzzard Before Breakfast

At the top of the dead live oak
looms, black against the sunrise,
a presence whose long neck and meager head
protrude from the bulky folds
of a vast astrakhan coat.

Motionless extension of the lefthand branch, he
looks out over the canyon, then turns
indifferently toward the kitchen window.
I can almost distinguish red skin
above his beak.
Ponderously he rearranges his person onto a horizontal plane,
one wing lifted, turns into a gigantic paper bird
placed by Christo,
ready to take off in the next updraft.

Fruit swollen with poison, tree gall, wasp nest *extraordinaire,*
zapolote!
You are not really baleful or cruel but
a magician of transformations,
kin to cleaner fish and garbage men. Within you
cast off bones and last year's flesh
become warmth and feathers and upward soarings.

He turns his beak toward me, nods
Au revoir
and glides away.

Grackles

attentive to the morning light
arrange along telephone lines,
quarter notes on a staff
of bird gossip medley.
Wires sway under late arrivals
bony claws tighten to balance,
release to sidle,
quarter notes shift to rearranged melodies
and new pecking orders establish.

Goldfinches

Goldfinches swoop, gilt leaf ribbons
breezing from fence to treetop.
The molecules they knock askew vibrate
back into place, join currents of air
sifting through the fence rails. Urgent,
insistent corpuscles of color quicken
in the grain of feathers. Still
in the branches, the goldfinches sit,
poised on the brink of sunlight, ripe
pears, a flutter of taste in the air.

Hawk

Ripping through the early morning skies,
hazed green with pollen, the caustic cries
of crows batter me about the ears—
a scrambled squadron of four birds, their jeers
goading each other on in their attack
on a single hawk. They dive and jab at his back,
shoulders, belly, and eyes. Blinded, he
will be theirs, golden and bloody, set free
of this plague of beaks, this game of deadly odds:
four on one, dogs eat the loner.

The gods
will not descend to intervene here. The script
is set. I turn away; the hawk is whipped.
I walk out on the denouement, the final scene
with its lesson on survival. I had been
victim of knowledge enough for one day.

And then
I remembered being bullied time and again
on the grammar school playground.
I turned to face
the foe, yelled and clapped gunshots to chase
them off. They scattered in a flap and a squawk
or two, left me standing below the hawk
rising now in circles unaware
of justice or the ironies of fair
play, and certain only of the steady air.

before metaphor and without image

3 a m and my left knee aches
keeps me awake
while I'm writing a labor long detailed
poem which I hate
because while I'm taking time
to describe things
I'm afraid I'll forget
what I really want to say

at first light
I hear a thump on the glass door
a sparrow lies stunned
on the brick patio
a snail is sound asleep
on the inside of my window blind
and later around 7 a m
a coyote passes through my back yard
with the voice of a sandhill crane
caught in his mouth

hawk stopped by to rinse his wings
I told him I wish I'd left the door open
for the sparrow and how I heard
the snail in the night rattling my blind
and thought it was the wind
when I started to mention coyote
he told me to stop naming things
so I could hear who is speaking

hawk

in this place where spirits visit
I swallow silence
count secrets on a cricket's wing

a hawk ridges the valley of the bear-claw tree
watches dawn bend stillness
through a curtain of elk

I slip my bones between prairie grass
tell hawk it's a strange trail for me
but you're here he says
then sweats his feathers
so he can speak to the moon

House of Ten Hawks

There is a creel
of screeching
overhead,
skirting the swollen
toe of a careless sun,
raftered along the beamswell
and doorslammed wind,
tracing routes
of the air ant,
queening swarms
through ritual nimbus,
where talons tear
twenty holes
in a carcass
of sky.

There are thresholds
to nurture, hearthstones
to set in the last
firing of the sun,
angles to round at nest site,
trout flesh to separate
from windowbone,
in a house of ten hawks,
lampless as trees at new moon
that waver in retinal strands
under vigilant streams,
birded and sloth-beaked,
the split light of tempests
in their bolted wings.

A flash
in the prey-locked eye.
Swift struggle,
ascending,
ten meters high.

Growing a Bird

This fragile cage,
once a house of song,
still intact, kept

by the slow ebb of cartilage,
tinkles like marrowglass, hollow
where the light strays

through the delicate weave
of down and grass, clinging
and bursting through spring ribs

reaching across this season
of stillnesses, season that swallows
only the sound of song.

I wrap this gentle, empty
house in a bunting of bulbs,
burlap, a wet shroud of afterwarmth,

of no further interest
to worms who cool
their segments against

newly inscripted
stone and the hope
of fresher game.

And I know soon a raiment
of risen bones, burgeoning, in foliar green,
will bend against the breath of rain

recanting oaths under sky. Soon,
beneath the steady meters
staved by measures of light

and dark drums, pulsing the stalk
up through rich ochre,
high into blue tongues

trilling grace notes of red,
yellow, orange, maroon,
a miraculous bird: paradise.

Spring Haikoem

Whirring hummingbird
Feeds on morning's bright trumpets,
Marks stems on the notes,

Hovers horn to horn
In a prelude to summer,
Spreading melody

Sounding among staves
Of trebling blossoms, ringing
Like a glockenspiel.

Sun-chant concerto:
Bumblebee and timpani,
Crickets come bowing,

And beak for baton,
Hummingbird conducts me from
My symphonic sleep.

Haiku for Mourning Dove

So owlant the sound:
Baleful moaning wounds the dawn.
Sorrow starts early.

After Reading Peterson's Guide

I used to call them
Morning Doves, those birds
with breasts the rosy color
of dawn who coo us awake
as if to say love...
love...in the morning.

But when the book said
Mourning Doves instead,
I noticed their ash-gray feathers,
like shadows
on the underside
of love.

When the Dark Angel comes
let him fold us in wings
as soft as these birds'
though the speckled egg
hidden deep in his nest
is death.

Waiting for *E. gularis*

"An African heron was found on the northeast end of Nantucket Island...."
—*NEWS RELEASE*

"The sighting of the century...."
—*ROGER TORY PETERSON*

Exile
by accident
he came

against
all instinct
to this watery place,

mistaking it
perhaps
as the explorers did

for some
new
Orient.

This morning,
dreaming
of the inexplicable

I rise from sleep, smoothing
the sheets behind me
to match

the water-smoothed sand
silk
under my bare feet.

I walk past morning joggers
who worship in pain
the crucible of breath,

past dune and marsh
stockaded with eel grass
to this pond,

just as a breeze comes up
like rumours
of his appearance.

Teenagers in bathing suits
lounge here, fans
waiting for their rock star

E. gularis—even his name
becomes
an incantation.

The pond
is all surface
this cloudy day,

the dark side of a mirror
where nothing shows
until you stare enough

as at those childhood puzzles—
how many faces can you find
concealed here?

And there moving towards us
is the turtle's miniature
face,

and there the mask
the wild duck wears, stitching
a ruffle

at the pond's far edge
where now
the Little Blue Herons

curve their necks
to questions marks
(why not me?)

where in a semi-circle
ornithologists
wait

to add another notch
to their life
lists,

binoculars
raised
like pistols.

The Birds

are heading south, pulled
by a compass in the genes.
They are not fooled
by this odd November summer,
though we stand in our doorways
wearing cotton dresses.
We are watching them

as they swoop and gather—
the shadow of wings
falls over the heart.
When they rustle among
the empty branches, the trees
must think their lost leaves
have come back.

The birds are heading south;
instinct is the oldest story.
They fly over their doubles,
the mute weathervanes,
teaching all of us
with their tailfeathers
the true north.

Random Sightings

Roger Tory Peterson and I

We had a chat today about how illustration
Often outmaneuvers the effects of sunlight.

Before I met Roger, I could not correctly identify
The second- and third-year gull plumages.

Did I tell you he is not much of a conversationalist?
When he does speak, people crick. Listen—

He imitates the calls of the eiders.
On this trip he hopes to learn more about pipits.

Though Chinet bowls are set out for the apricots,
He requests his on top of his oatmeal.

As if we weren't already fortunate to have had
This chance, Roger, as it happens, is

An avid lister. He says the only other
Feathered beings are angels, rare but regular.

What other field confers such fame from writing
One book? Roger's art with words

Endows with flight-song, habitat and range
The field marks he discovered first.

Secure in style and current accomplishment,
He still hears acutely as ever.

Murre Eggs

Unlike the parents' black and white, they're bright,
Alone, and pyriform. They wait their part.
Had Jackson Pollock held them in his sight,
He might have feared that nature copies art.

The egg-collector finds an unmarked white
Rarely. As he dangles on his long rope,
He sees an ecru splashed with madder, light
Cobalt green, a gold-flecked maroon. His hope

Is vertical and brief. They in their shape
Stay put, or circle in on the thin ledge
If a wind rise. Nor do their marks escape
The murres who left them fog-bound at the edge.

We turn in circles too. Sometimes it's wise.
We learn to reckon and be recognized.

Seventeen-Line Sonnet

Now we go back to the popcorn ceiling
And the seamless sky, exchanging gray for blue,
Reality for illusion. Or is it the other way?

Now you are seventy-five, but are you feeling
Much different than you did at twenty-two?
I don't think so, although I'm sure you do.

Now we go back to the orange tree and now
The six-foot rose. And will the lilac bloom
That missed the Appalachian frost and gloom?
The tristful mourning-dove, the raucous crow,
The arrogant raven and the flirtatious finch
Now will replace the pigeons of Broadway.

Now crawls the continent under inch by inch.
So crawl the years, still with felicity.

Now I adapt your written words to mine,
For in this way we once again combine:
Be good to my love! Take care of her for me!

The Rooks at Haworth

Bronte Parsonage—Yorkshire, England

Even ordinary things
lie enshrined
An old comb, pigments in a paint
box, dry as stone
Emily's lamp, no larger
than her hand, still seeks
the stair—small bedrooms where
children pressed pale against the glass
look down
to the churchyard
there, mothers and sisters lie
entombed.

Wind still blows
lapwing and moorland
grouse survive amid the gorse.
Over rainy heath ghost rooks
fly, past peatsmoke from stone
chimneys, sluice down the darkening sky,
settle, random chessmen
on the graveyard's shouldering tablets.
Keening, croaking
shrouded as old women
hunched over candles
they pulse out again and again
in ancient argument with death
a raucous distrust
an abiding enmity
against the slippage
of day...

Pelican Perch

I perch on my piling
an awkward wild thing
balanced by waddling
webbed feet
gray skin spun
between four mighty fish-ripping claws

I could slash you with these talons
pierce you with the razor hook
on the tip
of my baggy bill
shock you with the power of one
outstretched wing
if you get too close

I'll just wait on the wharf
nestle in my feathered pile
sunken neck between wings
white tuft rising on my crown
and watch you with steady yellow eyes

I'll command you to throw me that mackerel
or bass
from your lure
not in the water where those cormorants hunt
not beside me where those damn lyric gulls
scavenge and steal
but here
in my open, hungry, pink snapping sac

In younger days
I'd join that arc of fellow fliers
inches above the slapping spray
and plunge dive at sublime speeds
for rock fish and jacks
but it's easier to rest on this pier
now I just shovel bait bits into my pouch
and preen
at your feet

Day Full of Gulls

Slow as the tide, a lifeguard smooths
his gritty girl, and seagulls stand
and the shadows of clouds appear like pools
and the waves fall back on themselves like sleep.

Day full of gulls, a storm of gulls,
wheel within wheel of caw and sweep,
never seeing enough of them,
how they tilt the air, and glide, and ebb.

At noon in the surf some raucous boys
made them scream like themselves, wings batting bodies,
vicious for lumps of last week's bread.
Day full of gulls. A storm of gulls.

Now women cast out evening crusts
like a sowing of love, and fathers aim
bits plucked like cake crumbs from the loaf,
to be snapped in mid-air with stern elegance.

A girl in the drift of the sea edge leans
on tiptoe, skirts held up. A gull
ends flight, like an indrawn breath,
on the small of its shadow.

Sea Gulls

Two gulls
argue about a fish
flat-stepping
back and forth
avoiding
serious quarrel
while the marina cat
drawn silent
as a magnet
toward the smell
stops between them
at the spot
where the fish
flopped briefly
undecided which bird
to follow
and gullible
turns toward
the wrong gull
as the other one
like an under-sprung
shopping cart
bumps the fish
firmly along
the dock and
around the corner
settling the matter.

Swans

Seen from a distance, swans are more pleasing.
On the weir at Chester, where the Dee winds below city walls,
 I once saw five and fifty swans waddling, pulling out old
 feathers, or head beneath the water, examining food.
They fed, swam two by two, rose up with great flapping wings
 to skim across the water on their toes and settle down again,
 wrapping their wings about them and wagging their downy tails.

When the water lies clear and deep, theirs is the glass of
 fashion and the mold of form.
Where the stately Isis flows, there the grave swan dozes.
And who has not seen him in retired corners of the Thames,
 shedding brightness as he drifts?
Or, between moor and cliff, on Crag Lough's blue waters,
 swimming softly—a creature of snow and fire,
 songless, eternal.

Family Tour

The car comes to a stop, and Daddy's hand
Is raised for silence. "Listen," he says.
We listen for the expiring sigh of tire or engine,
For the voice of brigands crying Halt!—in French
Or Italian or Spanish, but there is only the wind
And some bird cheeping in the hedgerow.

"There it is again," he says. "Naturally,
They are in better voice at night."
Daddy has heard a nightingale.
Refreshed in mind and at heart, he
Starts up the car once more.

The nightingale is a retiring bird,
To be found in the neighborhood of
Chinese emperors and of my father.
Beneath his window on a noisy Roman street,
Nightingales sang every afternoon when he napped.
In lime trees by Paduan canals,
In almond groves from Cannes to Aix,
In the Abbot's rose garden at Mont-Saint-Michel,
Nightingales were singing when Daddy passed by.
Over the hills of Umbria and into Tuscany,
Across the river valleys of France and into
Spain, they followed him rapturously,
Darkening the air with song, and at Granada they
Welcomed him to those ruined halls in choral splendor.

Nothing since has quite equalled the Spanish trip.
Near Broceliande larks were singing;
There was a cuckoo in the woods at Guéhenno;
Swifts were migrating noisily in the Abbey grounds
At Hexham; and, on the Roman Wall,
Mother and I followed the wall,
Daddy the cry of the curlew.
But it was not the same thing.

So when he looks pensive and says he is thinking
Of all the letters he must write,
It is probably not true.
O nightingales of Granada, he hears your far-off warblings,
He sees those groves of Spanish cypress and Spanish loves!

Him

So far, all day, the road to Lake Darling
is empty. A flicker with a broken wing
steps down to cross. Now the driver
comes and sees. He stops, lifts
the bird up in his hand, which tightens
on its one question. Driving this way,
the man is directed to a woman who
can fix this, and he goes to her. That
evening, he tells his wife how the flicker felt
waiting in his hand,
the little orange on its head, feathers all
of-a-piece. In the next week, from inside, oh,
she sees her first flicker on the wobbling suet ball
and she tells him first thing, thinking, there,
something is done now, something has been passed
through, thinking her desire caused it, or
the flicker did, or him.

Elegy for Marion Peirce

drowned at birth, June 30, 1949

A small beating in the basement, then
a stunned swift in my hand, light as
light. Grief in the form of a hand
with a sick bird in it. No, not sick,
beaten against a wrong dark side, the inside,
then, exactly the length of my barely cupped hand.
In this way things fit, says the brain,
flinging memory at the true. It had
a little squat whale-head, the wet
eyes low in the sides, dull whale-colored
feathers all over, as if fastest possible
passage were beauty enough. It had a common
swift's legs; exquisite, rubbery bones still
snarled in pulp brought from the other side, clutching
and clutching and clutching. In this way things tire,
says the body. Even the open hand gets tired, tired even
of grief, even of the dry light you waited for
to wake you with its beating.

Longing

Yesterday filled with sound, today
the nest is still. A braid of dry
grass sways in the indifferent breeze.

I found a curious comfort
in the daylong ritual under the eave:
the finch pair swooping, in turn,
toward their brood, throats opening
to tender, craving beaks; eager
melodies of family life.

Worried about the neighbor's cat,
I pulled an old door from the shed
and laid it across the porch.
Instinct isn't lost to the childless—
no more than hunger,
or longing…
                    Now the female returns,
perches below the eave. Her tail bobs
to a familiar strain as one eye
searches the hollow nest. Is she, too,
feeling this sudden, abiding loneliness?

A last moment's hesitation, then
she lifts and sails away, leaving
her music in the air

My Swallows

For hours I sit here facing the white wall
and the dirty swallows. If I move too much,
I will lose everything, if I even breathe,
I'll lose the round chest and the forked tail
and the nest above the window, under the ceiling.

As far as shame, I think I have lived too long
with only the moonlight coming in to worry
too much about what it looks like. I have given
a part of my mind away, for what it's worth
I have traded half of what I have—

I'll call it half—so I can see these smudges
in the right light. I think I live in ruins
like no one else, I see myself as endlessly
staring at what I lost, I see me mourning
for hours, either worn away with grief
or touched with simple regret, but free this time
to give myself up to loss alone. I mourn
for the clumsy nest and I mourn for the two small birds
sitting up there above the curtains watching—
as long as I am there—and I mourn for the sky
that makes it clear and I mourn for my two eyes
that drag me over, that make me sit there singing,
or mumbling or murmuring, at the cost
of almost everything else, my two green eyes,
my brown—my hazel, flecked with green and brown—

and this is what I'll do for twenty more years,

if I am lucky—even if I'm not—I'll live
with the swallows and dip through the white shadows
and rest on the eaves and sail above the window.
This is the way I *have* lived, making a life

for more than twenty years—for more than forty—
out of this darkness; it was almost a joy,
almost a pleasure, not to be foolish or maudlin,
sitting against my wall, closing my eyes,
singing my dirges.

Mimi

For all that grackles are despised
I saw a baby grackle
walking on the red leaves
around my Honda. I chased

her from right to left, she ran
with the speed of a sandpiper, she ran
with the speed of a pigeon. I saw
she was a baby when she lifted

her wings—she looked like a chicken—
and I knew she was young when she turned
to wait for me. I think
she was playing, even when she stopped

to pick at a seed or a crumb,
walking from right to left,
sometimes running when I half
caught up to her, but never

flying away, that would be
the end of our game. I love
all species whose children are the size
of their own mothers, that means

the cowbird as well as the grackle,
that means the robin. I love
the rose that waits. I love
the tulip gorged with blood,

I love all pigs that live on
the shit of other animals.
I love the cardinal who spends
her life with the blue-jay. I love

the hatred between them. There is
a black and white cat who chases
my squirrels; I love how she climbs
my arbor vitae and drops

on the roof outside my bedroom.
I love her grief as I lift
my window to let her in.
Did I say the squirrel baited her?

What would I do if the grackle
stopped running? There was a pigeon
in Rome who refused to move;
I think she was dying, her eye

was lifeless. I was afraid
to touch her. The eye of the grackle
is like a flame, her heart
beats 400 times a minute.

I stuff my pockets with leaves.
What should I do? They sometimes
are wet one day, then dry
another. Some are so huge

they cover my plate. I'm listening
to La Boheme. It gives me
a second history. My grandfather
heard it in Poland. Puccini

was more a hawk than a grackle;
he hunted larks. His singers
were scattered on top of the leaves
raging and dying. All this is

unknown to grackles; they live
without much raging and die
without much singing. They spit
up blood with hardly a word.

There is no last great vanity,
no final sobbing, no amorous
thumping, no double sadness
in peculiar fifths. If they do sing

it is an ascending squeak,
more like a rusty hinge,
more like a grating. There was
a crow I knew sang Tosca,

she plunged her beak into
her ravager's breast, she cawed
with happiness, she gurgled,
but that was different. This sky

will have no moon till five
in the evening, we will have to
contend in the morning. I will
fall from the parapet first

or she can crumple a leaf up
for one of her letters. In my version
I would have let the politics
sneak in much more, that is

the edge love needed. I would have
modernized it—something
from after the war, either Nixon
or Senator Joseph disguised

as a scorpion; J. Edgar Hoover
getting his files together,
getting ready for his blackmail;
or in the other—that sweet other—

when Mimi dies I'd fall
under the hubcap, I'd sing
my last good song in the voice
I lost at thirteen, in the style

of Bobbie Breen; he was
a boyhood singer—all mothers
wept at his sound. I am
at this late date, December

1991, on a street corner
in Jersey City the poet
Rudolpho—I am a Rudolph—
and I am burying Mimi

who died by flying away
somewhere over a bakery
when boredom finally took her.
This is the truth though my music

makes light of it. I tore
a leaf for her and fasted
for fifteen minutes though nothing
was there. I felt some dread

but that gave way to sleepiness
and fluctuations of the mind,
mostly a dark red cardinal
that Puccini must have invented

for his own undoing, "alone"
in her redbud, "lost, abandoned,"
and—God—I hate to say it
but—only for me—a kind of

cross between a toucan
and a sparrow, doing his laments
at the top of his voice, his false one
to be sure, stabbing his wives

one by one—a specialty—
making his savage speeches,
writing his bitter letters
on his legal pads, a toucan

of anger, a sparrow of shame,
piling the words up, turning them
into poems, then dying
on *his* hill of leaves, a Rudolph

beyond all Rudolphs, Pagliacci
secundo, Siegfried der wanderer,
Tristan der melancholish, Alfredo
der ethical, der loyal, dear Mimi.

Hanging Scroll

I have come back to Princeton three days in a row
to look at the brown sparrow in the apple branch.
That way I can get back in touch with the Chinese
after thirty years of silence and paranoid reproach.
It was painted seven hundred years ago by a Southerner
who was struggling to combine imitation and expression,
but nowhere is there a sense that calligraphy
has won the day, or anything lifeless or abstract.
I carry it around with me on a post card,
the bird in the center, the giant green leaves
surrounding the bird, the apples almost invisible,
their color and position chosen for obscurity—
somehow the sizes all out of whack, the leaves
too large, the bird too small, too rigid,
too enshrined for such a natural setting,
although this only comes slowly to mind
after many hours of concentration.

On my tree there are six starlings sitting and watching
with their heads in the air and their short tails under the twigs.
They are just faint shapes against a background of fog,
moving in and out of my small windows
as endless versions of the state of darkness.
The tree they are in is practically dead,
making it difficult for me to make plans
for my own seven hundred years
as far as critical position, or permanence.

—If the hanging scroll signifies a state
of balance, a state almost of tension
between a man and nature or a man and his dream,
then my starlings signify the tremendous
delicacy of life and the tenuousness of attachment.
This may sound too literary—too German—
but, for me, everything hangs in the balance
in the movement of those birds,
just as, in my painter,
his life may have been hanging from the invisible apple
or the stiff tail feathers or the minuscule feet.
I don't mean to say that my survival
depends upon the artistic rendering;
I mean that my one chance for happiness
depends on wind and strange loyalty and a little bark,
which I think about and watch and agonize over
day and night,
like a worried spirit
waiting for love.

Pile of Feathers

This time there was no beak,
no little bloody head, no bony
claw, no loose wing—only a small
pile of feathers without substance or center.

Our cats dig through the leaves, they
stare at each other in surprise,
they look carefully over their shoulders,
they touch the same feathers over and over.

They have been totally cheated of the body.
The body with its veins and its fat
and its red bones has escaped them.
Like weak giants
they try to turn elsewhere.
Like Americans on the Ganges,
their long legs twisted in embarrassment,
their knees scraping the stones,
they begin crawling after the spirit.

Hinglish

Sacré Dieu, I said for the very first time
in my adult life and leaned on a tuft of grass
in the neighborhood of one green daffodil
and one light violet, and one half-drooping blue-bell.

I did a stomp around my willow driving
the cold indoors and letting the first true heat
go through my skin and burn my frozen liver.

I placed the tip of my tongue against my teeth
and listened to a cardinal; I needed at least
one more month to stretch my neck and one
for delayed heartbeats and one for delayed sorrows.

"Speak French," she said, and dove
into the redbud. "Embrassez-moi," I said.
"Love me a little." "I am waiting for the hollyhock
and the summer lily," she said. "I am waiting
to match our reds. Baissez-moi," she said,
and raced for the alley. "Here is a lily, my darling,
oranger than your heart, with stripes to match
and darker inside than you." "Parle Français,
mon cher; pick me a rose; gather roses
while ye may; lorsque tu peux." "Have you
read Tristan Tzara?" I said. "Suivez-moi,
there is a bee," she said. "Forget your mother,
Oubliez vos fils vos meres." Her voice
is like a whistle; we used to say, "what cheer,"
and "birdy, birdy, birdy." There is a look
of fierceness to her. She flies into the redbud
without hesitation. It's easier that way. She settles,
the way a bird does on a branch; I think
they rock a little. "Nettles are nettles," she says,
"fate is full of them." "Speaka English," I say

and wait for summer,
a man nothing left of him but dust
beside his redbud
a bird nothing left of her but rage
waiting for her sunflower seed
at the glass feeder.

"A single tear," I say.
"My tear is the sky you see it," she says. She has
the last word. Halways. A bird is like that. She drops
into the hemlocks. Her nest is there. It is
a thicket at the side of the house. "I hate
the bluejay," she says. In Hinglish. She flies to the alley
and back to the street without much effort although my yard
is long as yards go now. How hot it will be
all summer. "Have you read Eluard?" she says.
"He avoided open spaces; his poems
were like my bushes and hedges; there in the middle
of all that green a splash of red; do you like
'splash of red'? His instrument was the wind.
So is someone's else." She has a flutelike
descending song; when she speaks French the sky
turns blue. "'On sand and on sorrow,' he said. He talks
just like you. He had a small desert too;
he had an early regret. There is a piece
of willow. I am building something. I'll speak
Hinglish now. I love simplicity.
I hate rank." "Little wing of the morning," I say.
"In the warm isles of the heart," says she.
"I hold the tenderness of the night," say I.
"Too late for a kiss between the breasts," says she.

Sitting on my porch,
counting uprights, including the ones on my left
beside the hammock, including the ones on my right
beside the hemlock,
reading Max Jacob,
speakin' a Hinglish.

Roseate Spoonbill in Telephone Pole Aviary

after twelve years, still people shy

Lunching al fresco
in their facsimilated marsh
they unloop sinuate necks
dip ovate-tipped beaks
splayed toes firm
like flattened spiders
hinged spoons snap
    open   shut

These gawky hunched-up birds
pastelled like a Fragonard
                freeze
as I step over the barrier

From the water's edge
  from the simulated copse
    from the feeding basin—
      a hollow slapping
        like a massive wave of applauding palms
      signals a great pearly rise:
    unshod air-borne ballerinas
  lanky legs outthrust float
up   up   to tree-top bleachers

and my mesmerized eye
    rides one porcelain-pink plume
        floating earthward

My vanished self lost in the rosy mist
    I clutch my nascent moment
        in this feather

Marabou Stork

in Islam, a sacred bird
in Europe, a good-luck presence

The black-tented bird
studies his image
in the pond.

Not handsome as his white brethren
nor exotic as his scarlet ibis cousin
but in black frock coat
back-thrust tails   white waistcoat
he carries himself proudly
lance-beak piercing the air
striding toward the hill

Like a child smitten with a slide,
who repeatedly mounts the ladder
to glide ecstatically back to the ground,

he half-runs up to the peak
pauses to stare outward
then his black cape fully unfurled

an avian batman, he sails down—
and again   and again
almost flying

finally sated, fully exercised
he struts back to the corral
seats himself sedately against the embankment
legs stretched out like a senior citizen
sunning in the Santa Barbara Zoological Gardens

Marabou means "holy" in Arabic.

Ballet Impromptu

Ugandan Gold-Crested Cranes:
ballerinas attending their
ballet-master's command

sur les points! Corps de ballet!
avançez!   grands jetés!
snowy capes unfurled
with an ecstatic rush
on hidden springs   surge
forward on toes

lift off   leap and
land   leap and bounce
air-borne rapture
on invisible trampoline
drunk on the taste of
innocent merriment

a breeze-skirmish-caress
riffles white pin-feathers
into rippled sea-foam wavelets
Do what I do
wing-tilts the leader
and they do, and I join in

keyed to the buoyancy of
rise and fall (I rise and fall).
One dancer pauses just
enough to stretch her long neck
toss back shimmering crest
and howl, not unlike a night

prowling concupiscent Tom   then
with a hoist and a flap runs daintily
to rejoin the troupe reveling in their
secret Hallelujahs.

At the zoo

Japanese sacred cranes

One bird sleeps
head under wing
while another preens itself

Sun rays dance
reflecting lights
on leaves and falling feathers

Shadows are frames
brushed in ink
black strokes upon a painting

Wild melodies

Today the wind
        after yesterday's rain

A humming bird
        tests the cover of pine
        pauses   mid-air
        and looks
in my window   climbs the light
and is gone

Touch of a Bird

Small body wings
        from tree
to the narrow sill outside
my window
Inside
a vase with yellow stalks
of grain transparent
            in the light

Tap-tap
on the glass   and again
tap-tap
          A closeness
in the twist of head
from side to side,   then
        quick fly-away
            and silence

Haiku

Look!
on freshly fallen snow
hieroglyphics
sparrows were here

pterodactyl

in this half light before dawn
a pterodactyl
wings the soft
dark air
past my face

i'm adrift in this
foreign place
no more at home
than the wingéd reptile
who flew the earth

until time struck
his ragged gavel
dismissing her
like a case

Condor

Your wings remember another sky
lost to us now, and so we need you,
survivor of power lines, bullets
and strychnine.
You are breeding again
in zoos, they release you
to the Sespe, they set out
carcasses and train you
like dogs to eat that meat
and no other.
Is it enough to feel
the air rushing past
your wings?
Does this echo
of the life you were born to
satisfy your bones,
or are you sorrowing,
like us, for the past
that haunts our sleep?

Hummingbird

Liquid energy lighting
on frantic red—
Summer fades against
your iridescent green,
your tiny blue heart
the center of flame
melting flowers.
You burn straight and true
even as you flicker
unpredictable as love.
How long do you live?
And do you change
from old to young
and back again
as you hover against
the sky, and vanish
in the thicket of leaves
that hides your
whispering nest?

A Quest for Cranes

The cranes were dancing a cotillion
as surely as it was danced at Volusia.
In the heart of the circle several moved
counterclockwise...the group attained
a slow frenzy.
—Marjorie Kinnan Rawlings

Mercury finished writing the alphabet
when he saw cranes form letters in the sky.

The poet Ibycus was murdered at sea.
The murderers were found by cranes
that followed their ship.

In Chinese legend, dead souls ride
the crane's back to heaven. In Japan
a crane brings longevity and peace.

Zen Master: Why do you want to see a crane?
    To dance. To ride one's back to heaven.
How do you know they exist?
    One of our party heard them at night,
    trumpeting as they flew.
Maybe your friend was dreaming.
    Maybe everyone is.
Did you see a crane?
    No, we saw other things.
    An owl who lives underground.
    A light brighter than the sun.
    An eagle eating a crow.
But no cranes?
    We are not ready for cranes.

Chicken Love

When it became apparent he would leave me,
I took a chicken from the flock,
held it upside down and stroked its head,
that it would lie docile beneath the axe.
The children cleaned it on the porch,
unaware of what the death forecast
despite the throat constricting stench.

One by one I killed the fowl. I simmered
them for hours in herbs and wine,
transforming the bloody sacrifice
into something we could swallow.

One hen was crippled. Her knees buckled,
her bloody toes clawed in. Her gimpy lurch
won the heart of our old cock.
Side by side they pecked about the knoll,
roosted together underneath the oak,
hastened slowly to the kitchen screen
for table scraps, the rooster tempering
his proud steps to hers. When every other
chicken had been killed, I let the couple be.

Birdwatchers in Mexico

A green bird, I said.
There, across the river.
You scanned. I see it too.
Let's move up.
We slogged through sand,
reached the verge.
Look! I cried. In that dead tree.
You rushed beside me, focused,
and we saw them—three green parrots,
yellow beaks, red eye rings.
A draft of air, a gust of luck,
something flushed them—
with hoarse squawks they surged,
circled, flashed crimson tails.
The leaves took wing and joined them,
screeching, air whipped and flailed
to green froth. They merged,
flew back within the brush;
but still, those grating cries.
Then silence, and the river.

For a Friend Who Asked Why I Watch Birds

It has all the thrill of the hunt
and I am a hunter,
my trophy fragments of color
flashed on the retina,
each feather perfectly set.

I hunt for the source of song
deep in the crown of a tree.

It is condensed like poetry.
Focused so intently on the twig
aflame with a fleet thing,
each dash of light changes the view
and quickens the heart of the viewer.

Revealed in glances
from branch to branch, a wingbeat
of time, a dart in the air,
a parting of leaves and the bird,
finally seen,
fuses song and light and movement
into grace.

Nightwatch

Nightwatch

Just before dusk
The great horned owl gliding
Cloud silent across the lawn
Lofts to a high dead branch
Among the knobcone pines.

Muffling wings about him
Like a wizard's cloak he turns
His tufted head from side to side
Gathering the failing light
Into his golden eyes.

Above a garden struck
To sudden fearful stillness
This artful night lord waits
With ears attuned, for dark to claim
The memory of his shadow.

At dawn his perch is bare
Beneath it, neatly packaged
Feathers, fur and bone.
My tame grey squirrel is missing
From a garden full of song.

A Haiku

a clear sheet of sky
calligraphy of blackbirds
written and erased

A Tanka

eyes alight with pride
he brings me five speckled eggs
jewels for my praising
deaf to the wood thrush's cries
amazed his treasures wound me

A Senryu

two a.m. the drunk
fumbling for his front door key
tries to shush the owl

The Ears of the Owl

The owl clings to the pine branch,
as the blind sky gathers around him
the hours beyond midnight, moonless,
drenched in darkness. In the still
cave of the sky domed above him,
the owl hears the dewdrops merging

on the leaves and stem of the creeper
and sparks in the air fired by whispers
of crickets. In the distant bottomland
he hears swallowing in the throats
of listening mice. He turns his head

and in the field under his talons
he hears the dry rasp of maple leaves
under the rabbit trembling motionless
above his own footprints. The owl
releases the branch and falls
into the opening mouth of blood.

The Wings of the Owl

The stretched wings of the owl sing
weightless over domes of air, the weight
of cold rain eddying under camber. The stiff
rocking of splayed feathers slips the wind
rippling down his sides. The driven sleet
dances across his back, slips sizzling

to leaves grounded, the platters of ice
in the ruts of the logging road. His tight
joints stiffen in the coil and shudder
of snow swept back from the bluff.
In a flattened glide, his wings flick
frost from the brows of moss, the thin

tarnish of lichen on granite. A twist
of muscle brakes him into the clatter
of branches, into the shape of the tree
trunk he gathers around himself. He leans
against the socket of a limb and settles
into the mottled fleck, grain, and stripe

the cells of his feathers have held memorized
for centuries. His eyes close, leaving
the trees empty around him, fragile
in the sea of yellow light, still pale,
but sharpening. He sleeps, dreaming
the shadow of blood drained from the sky.

Peace

From the bare trees the crow talks
a clatter of wickets. In the stolen
light of the moon he nurtures his vision
of the world creatured with ground-crawlers
drunk with the vision of their bones
indestructible, doomed to have him teach them
the last lesson. By the dawn star his wing
plows the mist. In the stiff heat of noon
he gathers his brothers and sisters to jeer
at the dwellers in the vast leafless spaces,
harvesting noise in bushels. They fill
the restless branches with dark punctuation
and hoard the word given them by the molecules
governing the tincture of feather, the perfect
composition of vessel, eye, the striated threads;
and when the world rolls over to play dead
the last time, crows and cohorts will flock
the sky black, and in the sullen night
they create, they will scream *pax, pax, pax.*

Crows

Crows rattle the winter branches,
and scatter into the hollow
wind like black shrapnel, twisting
a funnel of ragged shadows over
another maple as they fall, suddenly
converged on target: a hawk,
hunkered down on a small branch
close to the trunk, his shoulders
twitching, head bobbing to fake
clear of the crows' beaks, flashes
of obsidian lightning aimed at his eyes.

For the crows this is sport,
a diversion for bullies. They scrawk
and clatter 'till they tire of the game
and settle in another tree; then the hawk
rises, in that slow-motion liftoff
his wings require, and wheels away.
In this charade no one loses, no one
wins, though the hawk soars above them,
full of grace, refusing to give up
one scrap of humiliation.

Crow

You swerve off the telephone pole
making that ungodly racket
hoarse-throated
reiterating impudent nothings
rudely flapping across my garden
ignoring me
signaling your companions
with your raucous caw

You're a bow-legged misfit
waddling through my field
straight man
on the vaudeville circuit
done up in your dress suit
with the pants cut off too short

And yet I love you best of all the birds
because you transport me
to the pine trees
behind my Grandmother's house
where I hear you
cawing   cawing

Owl

How cool   how cool   how cool
how cool and cautious the owl   hiding deep
hiding   deep in fronds   dense fronds
dense fronds of the palm tree   the cool owl
hiding in the palm tree   fronds so dense
so dense no one can see him   no one can see him
solitary in dense fronds   sleeping solitary
solitary in the dense palm fronds   all day long
day long   till the night   the dark night
the cool owl can see   his eye in the night can see
in the night   his eye in the dark can see
the tiniest creature   the owl can see the tiniest creature
moving   tiniest creature moving in the dark night
the cool owl's wings so light   so light in the dark night
his wings light as milkweed spore   his flight light and silent
in the night   wings in the dark so light and silent
wings so silent   the mouse moving in the field
cannot hear   so silent the tiniest mouse moving
cannot hear the cool owl's flight   cannot hear the silent swoop
talons spread wide   sharp talons spread wide   wide
the cool owl   silent in flight   sharp talons
spread wide   wide   to capture the tiniest mouse
moving in the field   owl's talons spread wide   wide
to kill   to kill   to kill
owl silent   wings light as milkweed spore   silent in the night

Night Vision

By the side of the road and
all in slow motion   seen
from one corner of my eye
something
moving

then   come the lifting   wings
the feathers
almost brushing my breath
my sigh
escaping

and the Great Gray Owl unfurls
sideslips the hood of the car
enters the deeper dark
on the other side
like an echo repeating
all in slow motion

again
and again

The Owl

It's his eyes
that you can't forget.
He is seeing through
darkness to the death
of a mouse.
He doesn't breathe, blink.

His claws have locked
him onto a branch.
He is wearing a coat
of feathers to hide
the turn of his thoughts.
All the trees
here become skeletons.
Only their shadows bow.

The gravity in his heart
is pulling the forest
closer so he can
focus on the smallness.
A toad inside
his stomach is, at last,
turning into an acid.

This is how the owl's
mind must turn.
This is how it is
to be so awake the mind
is too large for a skull,
eyes almost lidless.

The intensity of the will
burning down
to the hottest coal.
His eyes set the forest
on fire, the dark fire
that even the moonlight
cannot put out.

Chicken Yard

The fox's thoughts
enter the chicken yard.
They slice like wind
on its way to nowhere.

The barn is red again
like clean blood.
And the corn scattered
here that makes the hens
peck greedily
never repeats its fear:
eat or be eaten.

Now the white hens
are satisfied with their
glowing fat and feathers.
They cluck to make
a stuttered noise and do
not understand they
move the light
in the fox's eye.

His brain is tight now
like a small room
that reason and terror
must share.
And his teeth go before
him and know what
he has not yet seen.

His hunger is opening
again like a clearing
where other desire is shoved
back into the woods.
The clearing is this
chicken yard, dotted and
blinking and teasing.
These bits of stars he,
on his way to forever,
must reach and grab.

Terror Triptych

The great bald unblinking bird opens
its gall studded beak   folds forward
both scaled blue wings   but is unable
to envelop me   barely beyond reach
arms pressed against my nipples
erect in the hot wind whipping
my nakedness
                    whirling down a long cobbled road
converged at a point that cannot be
seen   on the lower left corner I trip
on a scall-scalped crone   crouched over
an infant gargoyle   she sucks its cornea
                    sprawled at the gessoed edge   which
like an eye seeking light   I try to grasp
the landscape narrows   claws extended the bird
closes in   the crone unsated   has turned
toward me   and I cannot crawl off
the canvas

Bird Watch

A snowy egret follows me
and stares
way beyond rocks too slippery
to get a foothold

I think it is my mother

I cannot reach her
She never gets close

Sometimes she leaves the tidelands

I see her watch unblinking
from the roadside
wary at the edge of a culvert
or afar in a field of baby's-breath

I like her looking
and the way she lifts
and flies

just after the setting sun tears to shreds
clouds rising like a dark raiment
from the waters

flies to join the horizon
bent by twilight

Joan Fallert

After Being Struck Dumb by a Mob Burning and Looting Itself

Say I was the color of lichen, of wood,
could sit on a limb high in a tree and never
be spotted;
turn my head and see even the smallest,
the least thing move, move behind or
in front of me.
Say I could glide into night without
seeming to stir the air, still as spent breath,
swift, taloned, silent;
                                        a perfect predator,
                                        indifferent to despair
as pressure that builds, finds a fault and ruptures
the earth's crust, that hurtles hot winds down canyons,
fanning flames on their way to the sea;
                                        indifferent as nature everywhere,
                                        a perfect predator
leaving no trace but regurgitated pellets
of matted fur, teeth, bits of bone and
tiny blanched skulls.

The Heron's Dream

The heron who comes to me
was born
not in the cool center
of my unknowing
but high in a eucalyptus
in the center
of a parking lot at a public beach

the snack bar   bait   suntan lotion stench
permeating the air
before she unstuck her eyes and saw
foam cups   crushed bottle caps
wadded towels   umbrellas hoarding the shade
cars gunning their motors
and the slough between highway and sea
where she landed
when she finally flew

always slightly aloof
thrown into profile beside a cliff
reflected in the water or hidden
in the tall trees banked on the opposite shore

She dreams she calls for me like a school child
I come out on the porch
warmly dressed against the wind
climb upon her back
not like Mother Goose
or Dorothy's witch astride a broom
but leaning along the length of her neck
my legs tucked above her heart
out of the way
of the flap of her great wing

We soar   abandoning
cup-shaped anemones waving purple tentacles
the thorny berry bush
a walking stick clinging to its brittle twig
past butterflies and wild geese flying home
through clouds heaped
a great berm
dusted with shades no one else can see
mauve   chartreuse   gauzy greens twining
like ribbons

into the still blue
spiraling like the Fiend
thrusting his way out of Chaos
to a world she wants
to be
a perfect pendant
hung like Milton's universe
from the Empyrean

All night together
we glide   glad
and never light
Next day when I walk
by she doesn't blink
an eye

Wanderer

Calling
each to each, each
lifts and the great V drives
a wedge in the late autumn sky.
Snow Geese

flying
south, south to feed
and nest, ride the thermals
mile after guileless mile without
resting.

Coupled
for life they fly,
fly sometimes past midnight
into day, bills opening and
closing

slightly,
ceaselessly, necks
straight, eyes clear, opened wide,
fly toward the place they know they must
go to

and I
with no place to
be drawn to of my own
watch, listen for a heartland to
call me,

call me
back in the chill
air to somewhere which can
make my pulse pound, powerful as
wing beat

heading
for the sweet ground
on which the wild goose knows
it will be able to set down
at last.

Geese Going North

They fight to be free of our earth,
legs dangling, drawn up in the driving air,
wings stroking the wind, beating its current beneath the keel
of the breastbone as they're borne
toward that loud height
where we find them this morning in full flight.

On an April morning they ride
our warm wind from the south,
so many that all I can hear is their cry—
Canada Geese and Blues and Snows,
thousands squawking in the sky
while they flash over fields that weathered the winter.

On into noon they pass
in formation along the flyway.
They flock down to feed,
attracted by acres of corn or barley,
eager to graze on fresh grain or grass.
Once more they climb the wind—

They soar like a man who has flown
free of his thought,
happy to shed his shadow,
his dark image drifting alone
on swift wings over the earth. Wings which carry
the clamorous speed of the birds

farther than eyes can listen
for their long calls flying
out of the day and the fecund land
where our flesh follows.
As though to enclose the cool lake
below their voices

a pine forest grows
more green and remote when it rises.
Geese glide through these trees to reach the shore.
At rest on the water, wide wings withdrawn,
they float over the lake in its last light,
blue pool of the soul that deepens with the night.

Owl Has Closed His Eyes

Owl has closed his eyes to the cold spell.
He will not be a witness to winter,
it appears to displease him. Moreover
he won't complain, he voices no comment
(though his toes are freezing).
Back toes braced, tense talons
biting a bare limb, Owl
could not sit more stiff or still
if he were stuffed and mounted.

Never mind that a north wind
arrived without warning
to spin the feathered weathervane
on each henhouse, catching the cocks
quite by surprise—those who woke
Rock Lake this morning with their icy cries.
Their ruling vanity ruffled, if not routed.
An amusing prank, you think?

Owl cares nothing about it.

Talking to Mockingbird

1

Sing, you nightbird,
as though the sun rose
in your throat

A night of music, your
startling repertoire: blackbird,
starling, cheeping sparrow
and sparrowhawk
raucous jay and parakeet
lost seagull   demented
joy of imprisoned canary
and the screech owl who always
takes the shape of death

Nightbird, you mock me

2

I have raised my hand
against myself   In my family
this is a tradition

I thought I could salvage something,
thought I could strike before the blow
the rain of blows

Empty niches
in the wall of rock
once were altars

Oh you nightbird,
how many times
have you witnessed this?

You call me away
from the ritual, the knife
stabs harmlessly
through saved air

3

Does the song contain
the death of song? In darkness
you leave no shadow
Where do you dwell
when you are not pitched
in the crown
of native olive
or whistling palmtree,
flinging your melodies

a handful of coins
tossed down the long
alleyway of night

4

Sing louder!
sometimes my night ear
can't hear you

Is this because
a tiny bone
was stolen?

5

Your notes rain over
devastated groves and down
back streets of the city
where the ones with bags
and sticks come humping,
collecting our pittance

Every now and then the moon
shows up among the refuse,
our hands seem silver, we
who cannot sleep,
who have spoken wild or arrogant
or treasonous things…

Tell me, Nightbird, can it be
fleeing you and seeking you
are the same?

Three Short, Two Long

At twelve each night it begins to trill,
three short two long, a nightingale maybe
but not so sweet or a mockingbird
but not so shrill

and when I finally locate its name
like the lover lost in the midst of growing up
or now nearing the turn of the century, the one
whose sweet words slipped off my ear,
I want to begin another poem, a sweeter one,

one not so shrill. There it is again,
four short ten long, no iambic pentameter,
no pattern I can count on or song to fathom
how the phantom cat got into the house tonight
as if this bird could even guess

but there it is again boasting its escape,
maybe trying to tell me through what unsealed crack
the cat snuck looking for a victim,
and when I snapped on the light pursuing a shuffling
of shells, it glared at me from the window ledge,

one foot next to the abalone, the other
between conch and clam, and with my scream
it became a black flame tearing from ceiling
to corner, clinging to thin dimity curtains,
then with the loss of all recourse it crashed

smashing my daughter's crystals and geodes,
the African violet's green leaves shorn
from their source, green tears in a mess of red clay.
With its pathetic belly-centered cry, I realized
all the beast wanted was the night

and this I could understand, this wrong turn
into a house of books and looks without a home.
Stepping between the shambles of its panic
to slide open the window for its escape, I managed
to purr there-there, in a blessed moment

able to give the cat something I could not
give myself, the fur at the end of its tail
softening my gaze stuck on the rim of the moon
along with the bird's erratic trill, something
I can count on afterall in the settling
that has no name, a song to take me far away
looking for my own.

Heron

Blue heron posing at slough edge
stalks burn-off rising in bellows
up over a eucalyptus break

its head jerking as if struck
with secrets eased up
from swamp bottom

I follow smoky spirals
eyes squinted hoping to see
or hear what it does

only utterly still
immobile for a solid second
I must capture on film

With camera ready for focus
the burn-off shoots out of frame
pulling the heron with it

leaving me posing
at slough edge with nothing
on the other side of my lens

except my last breath
                    tailing after

The White Heron

Each year, at winter's start
the white heron returns.

He watches from the marsh
as night descends on earth.

Beneath his wings, the sun
is hidden from the shore

Spared the dying season
in a world left forlorn.

Yet through the darkened reeds,
time stirs an old desire

As spring and fall together meet
in bird and fire.

The Sign is Zeta

The sign is zeta in a hunter's sky
where my flamingo flies
toward the waiting gun.

High over the horizon comes its cry
on flaming wings that rise
to embrace the sun.

Too late for return or retreat, its way
confused by the smoke and blaze
of the final flight

Zigzag it turns as it burns through the gray
like a scar of the face
of the parting light.

Then zero...as the ash-hissing sea
brings an echoing in relief
for beauty so brave.

Truly the waves wash up and over me
as the zodiac clouds sift peace
on the darkened grave.

One and All

A hummingbird sees
the jade trees in my garden.

He prays with his wings
for peace in the West and East.

With his beak he tastes
the same blossoms. They are sweet.

One sun, one sky praise
Buddha and Christ for the feast.

One wind, one rain bring
food and drink, that all may eat.

For moles, worms, snakes, bees,
we ask glory and pardon.

Hummingbird

He dangled in air, level
with my eyes, making a difficult
choice,
then lighted on a twig the color
of himself, two feet from my chair.
The whirr drained from his wings;
he was small as an acorn,
smaller than my thumb.
Did I summon him,
or did he come,
driven by weather to this sheltered place?

He dared me with his coral eye,
measuring my menace
against the gale outside the wall.
Whether I shared his world,
or he mine,
was not the question.
We were bound,
as separate leaves upon a vine;

marked time, kept truce
until the mountain blackened and the wind
let the oleanders go:
a bird, brief haiku
of a bird, and I—
judged less fearful
than an element—
sipping each other's presence
like the dew.

The China Hummingbird

this morning in the yard
doing my usual thing,
some serious thinking
pulling a weed or two,
I hear it suddenly again
soft as the dawn air
the sensuous sound,
the whisper,

China… China…

it's a mind mirage, I think
and I have the strangest feeling
that it comes from
that green hummingbird
you like so much,
it's been haunting me all morning.
now, smooth as silk
drawn out this time,

Ch… i…n… a…

please come back
please tell me

Final Passage

last night I felt the planet
give a lurch, come nearly to a stop
then shudder hard...perhaps
an earthquake far away...before
resuming steadily to fit into
its place among the stars.
today I found the reason for
this pause. in Florida a man
held in his hand a bird, a
tiny one named Orange Band
belonging to the species
Dusky Seaside Sparrow. this
little bird lived only on the
insects found in swampy places.
now the swamp where it and
all its fellows dwelt is gone,
destroyed by those who make the wars
who build their killing rockets
to whirl around the space
that birds should occupy
where death has won out
over life.
this little bird had whispered
out its final breath, another
species vanished from our globe
and now the weight our planet bears
is lighter by one bird.

Hawk

Sharp-eyed death flies low
this winter day
and from the deerpath
I feel his passing
in the rush of air

soft, sibilant is the sound

and in one breath I sense
I too am death
I fly between his wings
the same cold wind that bears him up
tears sharply at my face

the same cold chill knifes through my bones

the hawk's harsh need
has now become my own
and I too hunt the meadow

The Guest in the Garden

had this girl
brought the owl
with her

had this swift
flight been
her companion

on her way and
had she stooped
a little to not

be brushed by
giant wings
as she arrived

she asked me if
I had an owl
living in the oak

I answered no
that I had always
wished an owl

lived near and
now tonight at table
with our friends

we hear the
muted cry
an owl is near

and calls to
one of us   is
this the darker

shadow of the
girl who came to
be with us tonight

Hunters

the heron steps
with crafty stealth
quiet water
scarcely stirs
one by one
the spindly legs
move forward.

soft padded paws
slight, nervous flick
of tail, no blade
of grass stirs
even faintly.
the hunting cat
is prowling.

What If?

Seeing a great blue heron land,
unmoving, watching the ocean, I think:
what if birds had never been?

We'd cope somehow, despite lost song,
new ways would evolve of spreading seed,
cleaning crocodile teeth...but once begun

the thought of what's not so goes on:
no dogs? joggers? a clarified beach
without rocks or shells?—what if the waves

the very clouds and breeze held still,
and into that trance of stillness came
the first bird of the universe?—

coasting, landing, strolling, standing…
hugely lifting off again—
magnificent great blue heron.

Swans Themselves

Evening spreads; a shadow of light
grown large on the water. Clear day is gone
that held to the mind a swan-reflection,
ravishing glass, mirror of calm.

But swans themselves: they pick at their feathers
like one-legged beggars against a wall,
or bully ducks by the scruff of the neck,
or sleep on the banks, connubial,
their heads tucked tight,
like unbaked loaves.

I've seen them walking the highway, leaving
their pastoral function, plodding, ungainly,
whitened by dusk;
priests, defrocked.

But once swans rose above me, lovely,
ah they were lovely in heavy beauty,
soaring, length of their bone-necks pointing,
Nordic ships bearing tons of body
silently with them;
outsailing night.

The Vireo

for Virginia Prettyman

A girl stood, in the legendary light
of childhood, in Carolina, beside her father when he killed
a blacksnake in a tree
too high for either man or girl
to climb.
But snakes are climbers:
no height will keep them from
the eggs and young
of the "swinging birds," called so for their branch-hung
nests: the Vireo, whose name's source
remains mysterious.
Some call it greenfinch; greenlet.
It was not
that her father shot the snake, for she'd expect
that of her father.
Nor that it fell
forty feet, a wheeling
coil.
But that a fledgling
flew from its mouth as it died:
arced up the full light's course
of her cry: a saved bird, a vaulter
from the dark
that bent its bones and gummed
its wool of feathers: O
greenfinch: greenlet: fly,
fly from the darkness, swinging bird.
Fly from that narrow mouth
as evening settles
among the oaks.

ACKNOWLEDGEMENTS

Bartlett, Elizabeth, "The Sign Is Zeta." *Literary Review.*

—— "The White Heron." *Chandrabhanga*, India.

—— "One and All." *Crosscurrents.*

Bates, Julia, "Crow," "Owl," "Grackles." *One Road Down from the Wilderness*, by Julia Bates. Fithian Press, Santa Barbara, 1989.

Burden, Jean, "Hummingbird." *Taking Light from Each Other*, by Jean Burden. University Press of Florida, 1993.

Fraser, Meg, "hawk," "before metaphor and without image." *keep to the left of grizzlies*, by Meg Fraser. Fithian Press, Santa Barbara, 1994.

Glass, Malcolm, "Crows." *High Plains Literary Review.*

—— "The Ears of the Owl." *Yankee Magazine*, 1991.

—— "Hawk." *Southern Humanities Review.*

—— "Peace." *Art/Life.*

Greet, Ann Hyde, "Family Tour," "Swans." *Spring Eclogue*, by Ann Hyde Greet. The Golden Quill Press, New Hampshire, 1961.

Johnson, Sheila Golburgh, "Chicken Love." *South Coast Poetry Journal*, 1991.

—— "A Quest for Cranes." *The MacGuffin*, 1994.

—— "Birdwatchers in Mexico." *Voices International*, 1992.

Keithley, George, "Geese Going North." *Song in a Strange Land*, by George Keithley. George Braziller, Inc. Reprinted by permission of the author.

—— "Owl Has Closed His Eyes." *Earth's Eye.* Story Line Press. Reprinted by permission of the author.

—— "Fishing the Sky." *Uzzano.* Reprinted by permission of the author.

Kumin, Maxine, "Of Wings." Reprinted from *Looking for Luck*, by Maxine Kumin. With the permission of W.W. Norton & Company, Inc. Copyright © 1992 by Maxine Kumin.

Longo, Perie, "Heron." *Studia Mystica*, 1984.

MacCuish, Marianne, "The Rooks at Haworth." *Into Another Country*, by Marianne MacCuish. Fithian Press, Santa Barbara, 1990.

Owen, Sue, "The Owl," "Chicken Yard." *Nursery Rhymes for the Dead, Poems by Sue Owen.* Ithaca House, 1980.

Pastan, Linda, "The Birds." Reprinted from *An Early Afterlife*, by Linda Pastan, with the permission of W.W. Norton & Company, Inc. Copyright © 1995 by Linda Pastan.

—— "After Reading Peterson's Guide," "Waiting for E. gularis." Reprinted from *A Fraction of Darkness*, by Linda Pastan, with the permission of W.W. Norton & Company, Inc. Copyright © 1985 by Linda Pastan.

Peirce, Kathleen, "Elegy for Marion Peirce," "Him." Reprinted from *Mercy*, by Kathleen Pierce, by permission of the University of Pittsburgh Press. Copyright © 1991 by Kathleen Peirce.

Piercy, Marge, "Art for art's sake." Copyright © 1992 by Marge Piercy and Middlemarsh, Inc. First appeared in *Chiron Review*, Spring, 1992. Used by permission of the Wallace Literary Agency, Inc.

—— "Crow babies." Copyright © 1992 by Marge Piercy and Middlemarsh, Inc. First appeared in *Poets On: Offspring*, Summer 1992. Used by permission of the Wallace Literary Agency, Inc.

—— "We speak of seeing the heron as if there were only one." From *Mars and Her Children*, by Marge Piercy. Copyright © 1992 by Marge Piercy. Reprinted by permission of Alfred A. Knopf, Inc.

—— "The West Main Book Store chickens." From *Stone Paper Knife*, by Marge Piercy. Copyright © 1983 by Marge Piercy. Reprinted by permission of Alfred A. Knopf, Inc.

Roethke, Theodore. "All Morning," copyright © 1964 by Beatrice Roethke, Administratrix of the Estate of Theodore Roethke, from *The Collected Poems of Theodore Roethke*, by Theodore Roethke. Used by permission of Doubleday, a division of Bantam Doubleday Dell Publishing Group, Inc.

Shapiro, Karl, "Seventeen-Line Sonnet." *The Old Horsefly*, by Karl Shapiro. Northern Lights, Maine.

Smith, Macklin, "Roger Tory Peterson and I." *Appalachia*, 1992.

Snyder, Gary, "Magpie's Song," "Night Herons." *Turtle Island*, by Gary Snyder. Copyright © 1974 by Gary Snyder. Reprinted by permission of New Directions Publishing Corp.

Spacks, Barry, "The Vireo," "Swans Themselves," "The Strolling Crow." *Something Human*, Harper's Magazine Press, New York, 1972.

—— "Day Full of Gulls." From *The Company of Children*, by Barry Spacks. Copyright © 1969 by Barry Spacks. Used by permission of Doubleday, a division of Bantam Doubleday Dell Publishing Group, Inc.

—— "What If?" *Brief Sparrow*. Illuminati, Los Angeles, 1988.

Stern, Gerald, "My Swallows." *Poetry East*, 1988.

—— "Mimi." Copyright © June 1994 by The Modern Poetry Association. First appeared in *Poetry* and is reprinted by permission of the editor of *Poetry*.

—— "Hinglish." First published in *The American Poetry Review*, vol. 22 no. 1, January 1993.

—— "Hanging Scroll" and "Pile of Feathers" appeared in *Lucky Life* and *The Red Coal*, and are reprinted by permission of Gerald Stern.

Tremaine, Kit, "The China Hummingbird," "Final Passage," "Hawk," "Hunters." "The Guest in the Garden." *The Guest in the Garden*, by Kit Tremaine. John Daniel & Co., Santa Barbara, 1989.